The Amazing Students

of Venezuela

OTHER TITLES IN THE COLLECTION

The Wrestling Cholitas of Bolivia
Girls Rock Indonesia
The Mermaids of Jamaica

Written by
CLAUDIA BELLANTE

Illustrated by
ELIZABETH BUILES

The Amazing Students

of Venezuela

Crocodile Books, USA

An imprint of Interlink Publishing Group, Inc.

www.interlinkbooks.com

To Tina, so that in her future there are no borders
and much less wandering children.
Claudia

• • • •

To the rivers, may you stop being borders.
Elizabeth

First American edition published 2023 by
CROCODILE BOOKS
An imprint of Interlink Publishing Group, Inc.
46 Crosby Street, Northampton, Massachusetts 01060
www.interlinkbooks.com

Copyright © 2020, 2023 Grupo Edebé
Text copyright © 2020, 2023 Claudia Bellante
Illustrations copyright © 2020 Elizabeth Builes
English translation copyright © 2023 Interlink Publishing
Originally published in Spanish in 2020 by Grupo Edebé, Barcelona, Spain

Library of Congress Cataloging-in-Publication Data available
ISBN 978-1-62371-793-3 • hardback

Printed and bound in China on forest-friendly paper
10 9 8 7 6 5 4 3 2 1

MIX
Paper | Supporting
responsible forestry
FSC® C144853

Against All Odds was born out of the desire to tell our kids real stories of children living in distant places and facing unique situations.

The series talks about everyday gestures that in certain contexts can become important, even to the point of changing the course of events, defying prejudices and clichés, and redirecting our attention to often-overlooked problems.

All of the events described in these books really happened or are currently happening. Only the protagonists are the result of the poetic license; the author wanted to protect the identities of the minors involved in these stories.

There are bridges that connect and bridges that divide, bridges worth stopping at to admire the flowing river and bridges that need to be crossed quickly, without looking back.

There are very high bridges that cause vertigo and low bridges that you can jump off of and feel like a free bird in the air.

There are bridges that remain open day and night and bridges that suddenly close, leaving the birds caged and flightless.

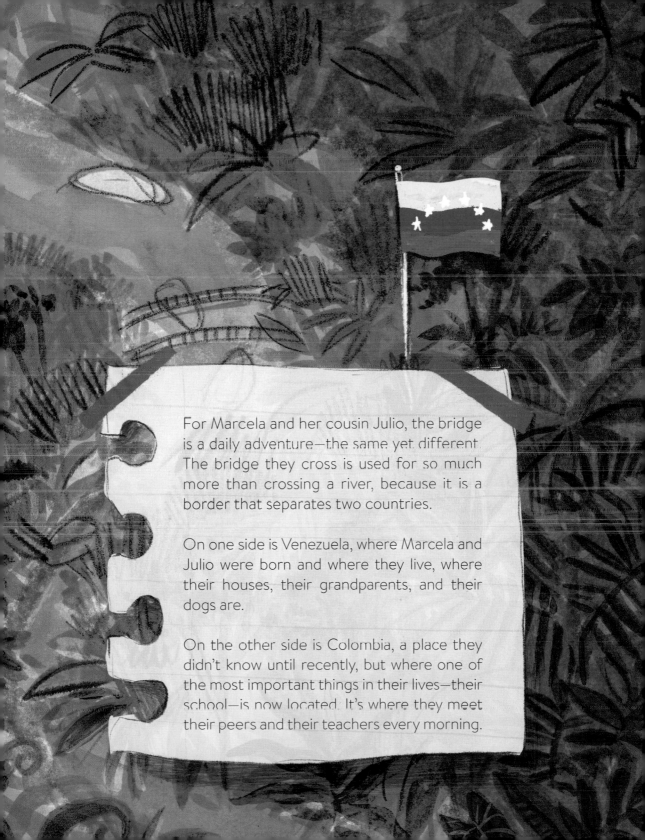

For Marcela and her cousin Julio, the bridge is a daily adventure—the same yet different. The bridge they cross is used for so much more than crossing a river, because it is a border that separates two countries.

On one side is Venezuela, where Marcela and Julio were born and where they live, where their houses, their grandparents, and their dogs are.

On the other side is Colombia, a place they didn't know until recently, but where one of the most important things in their lives—their school—is now located. It's where they meet their peers and their teachers every morning.

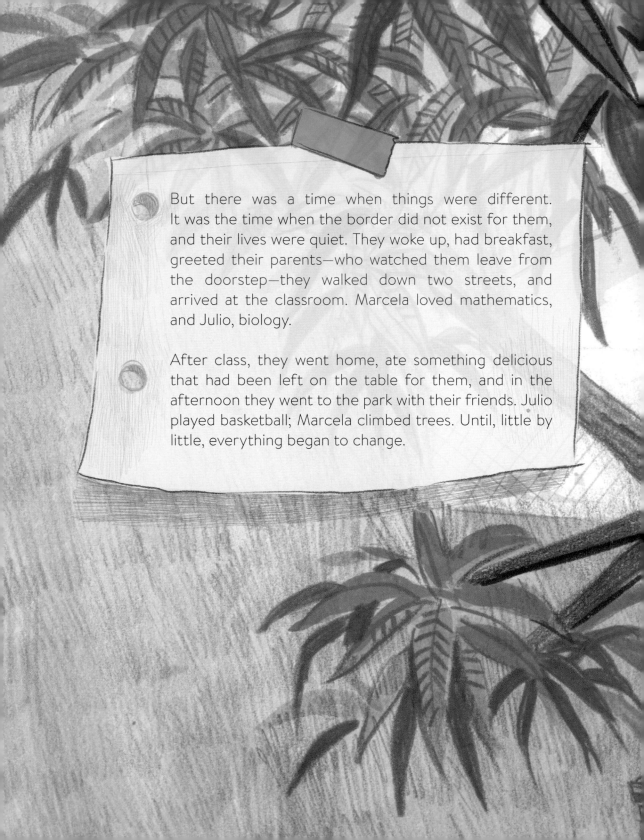

But there was a time when things were different. It was the time when the border did not exist for them, and their lives were quiet. They woke up, had breakfast, greeted their parents—who watched them leave from the doorstep—they walked down two streets, and arrived at the classroom. Marcela loved mathematics, and Julio, biology.

After class, they went home, ate something delicious that had been left on the table for them, and in the afternoon they went to the park with their friends. Julio played basketball; Marcela climbed trees. Until, little by little, everything began to change.

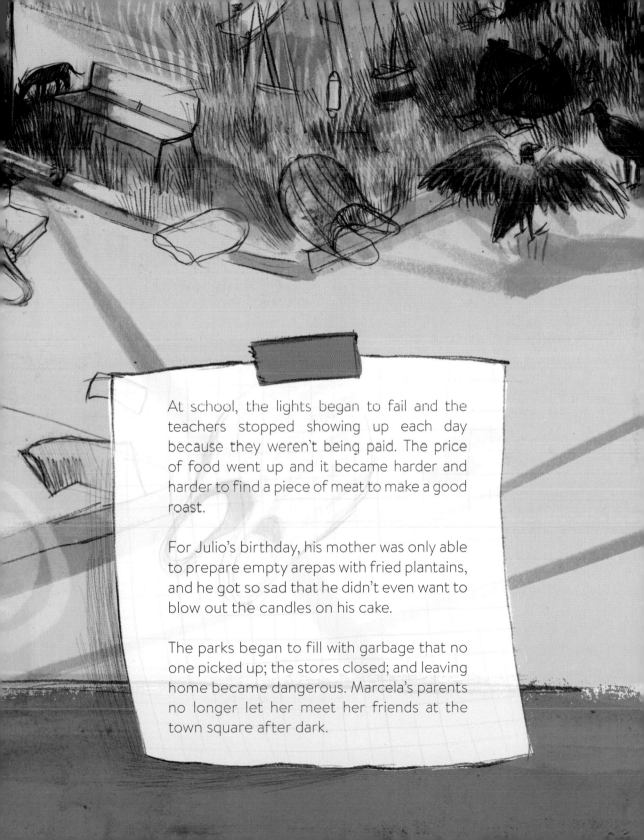

At school, the lights began to fail and the teachers stopped showing up each day because they weren't being paid. The price of food went up and it became harder and harder to find a piece of meat to make a good roast.

For Julio's birthday, his mother was only able to prepare empty arepas with fried plantains, and he got so sad that he didn't even want to blow out the candles on his cake.

The parks began to fill with garbage that no one picked up; the stores closed; and leaving home became dangerous. Marcela's parents no longer let her meet her friends at the town square after dark.

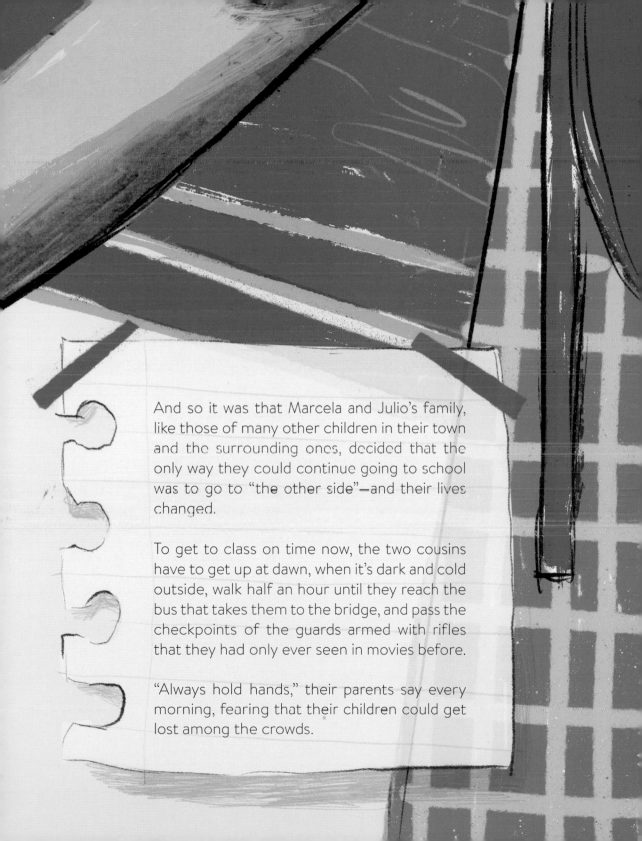

And so it was that Marcela and Julio's family, like those of many other children in their town and the surrounding ones, decided that the only way they could continue going to school was to go to "the other side"—and their lives changed.

To get to class on time now, the two cousins have to get up at dawn, when it's dark and cold outside, walk half an hour until they reach the bus that takes them to the bridge, and pass the checkpoints of the guards armed with rifles that they had only ever seen in movies before.

"Always hold hands," their parents say every morning, fearing that their children could get lost among the crowds.

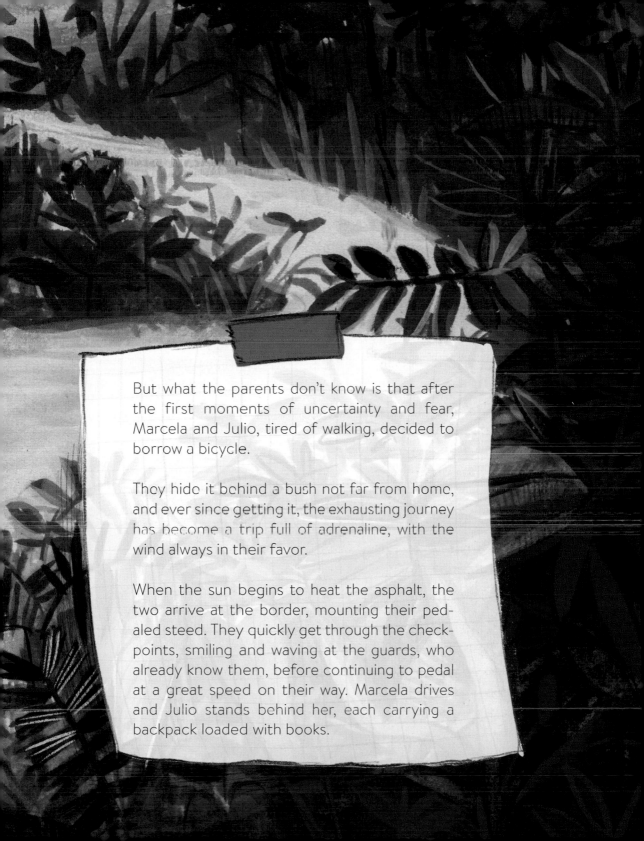

But what the parents don't know is that after the first moments of uncertainty and fear, Marcela and Julio, tired of walking, decided to borrow a bicycle.

They hide it behind a bush not far from home, and ever since getting it, the exhausting journey has become a trip full of adrenaline, with the wind always in their favor.

When the sun begins to heat the asphalt, the two arrive at the border, mounting their pedaled steed. They quickly get through the checkpoints, smiling and waving at the guards, who already know them, before continuing to pedal at a great speed on their way. Marcela drives and Julio stands behind her, each carrying a backpack loaded with books.

Like them, every morning thousands of people move from one country to another, from one life to another.

There are parents carrying their children to the doctor, women and men looking for work or shopping for food.

And then there are many students, like Marcela and Julio, with their plaid white-and-green uniforms or blue-and-red sportswear for gym class.

They cross alone, accompanied only by their dreams: to be a criminologist, like Valentina; a doctor, like Alfredo; or a pilot, like Maria.

On "the other side," school is different: there's more homework, and you have to study a lot. The kids complain, but they're happy, because they know that the more they learn, the more opportunities they'll have.

At first, some of the kids at school make fun of the newcomers—for coming from a different place, having another accent, and not always having ironed clothes.

But the Venezuelan children try not to feel bad, and thanks to the rap lessons they attend after school, they can express their feelings through music. Some of their songs have even become famous.

In the time Marcela and Julio have been going to "the other side," there have been difficult days, like when the border closed without anyone understanding why, forcing them to go under the bridge, get around the rocks in the middle of the river, take a boat, and cross through the tall grass.

They often arrived with soaking wet clothes or without a shoe, and sometimes, when they were too tired to get all the way back home after class, they would stay at one of their classmate's houses.

But amid these hardships, they've made new and profound friendships.

Marcela's best friends are Blanca, who is Venezuelan, and Marcos, who is Colombian. Next year, Blanca plans to meet her aunt in the United States, while Marcos will go to university in a big city in Colombia.

Marcela does not know what she'll do, because her parents own a small shop in the village they don't want to leave. She would like to continue studying, and since she's getting such good grades, she's applied for a scholarship.

Julio still has two years of school ahead and hopes that by the time he graduates, his country will be beautiful again, with many celebratory *asados*, schools full of interesting things to learn, and without a single child needing to cross a border alone to accomplish their dreams.

Terre des hommes

Proteggiamo i bambini insieme

This book has been made thanks to the support of Terre des hommes Italy, a foundation dedicated to protecting children from all forms of violence and abuse, guaranteeing their rights to health education.

In Norte de Santander, the region of Colombia on the border with Venezuela, Terre des hommes Italy is working to relieve the emergency of migrants: they run a canteen that offers 800 meals a day, a center for legal and psychological assistance, and a welcome spot for mothers and newborns.

For more information, visit www.terredeshommes.it

AUTHOR'S NOTE

I traveled to the border between Colombia and Venezuela with Terre des hommes Italy in June 2019, just a week after the reopening of the border that Nicolás Maduro closed in February 2019.

I have seen thousands of people cross the bridges that separate the two countries. Through Simón Bolívar, the longest and most famous bridge, some 28,000 people crossed every day. Approximately 25,000 returned to Venezuela at night, but at least 3,000 left their country forever every day. The area known as Norte de Santander, on the border, has always been one of the most dangerous in the region, controlled by Colombian guerrillas and paramilitaries now in conflict with Venezuelan armed groups. The huge flow of Venezuelans since 2015 has complicated the situation, and one of the risks migrants—children and adults alike—face is being drafted into the armed forces. According to data from the Interagency Coordination Platform for Refugees and Migrants (R4V), in August 2022, the Venezuelan Refugees and Migrants in the world were 6,805,209.

During my trip, I met and spoke with dozens of boys and girls, on bridges and in schools I visited on the border. They told me how their lives have changed, the effort it takes to get up at dawn, the dangers they face daily, but how happy everyone is to keep studying. My greatest admiration goes to their parents, who have lost everything but refuse to sacrifice the future of their daughters and sons.